My recipe book

This recipe book belongs to

_____

_____

Helpful information

Measurement equivalents

Liquid measures	Fluid ounces	Metric
1 teaspoon	0.16	5 ml
1 tablespoon = 3 teaspoons	0.5	15 ml
1/4 cup = 4 tablespoons	2.0	59 ml
1/3 cup = 5 tablespoons+1 teaspoon	2.7	79 ml
1/2 cup = 8 tablespoons	4.0	118 ml
1 cup = 16 tablespoons	8.0	237 ml
2 cups = 1 pint	16.0	473 ml

Dry measures	Ounces by weight	Metric
3 teaspoons = 1 tablespoon	0.5	14.3 grams
2 tablespoons = 1/8 cup	1.0	28.35 grams
4 tablespoons = 1/4 cup	2.0	56.7 grams
8 tablespoons = 1/2 cup	4.0	113.4 grams
12 tablespoons = 3/4 cup	6.0	170 grams
16 tablespoons = 1 cup	8.0	226.8 grams

This is American standard measures, approximate measurement equivalents.

Nutrition Facts (Serving size 100 grams)

Food	Protein	Carbohydrate	Fat	Calories (kcal)
Eggs (chicken)	12,7	0,7	11,5	157
Cheese (Dutch)	26,8	0,0	27,3	361
Milk	2,8	4,7	3,2	58

Yogurt (1,5%)	5,0	3,5	1,5	51
Dairy butter	0,6	0,9	82,5	748
Chicken	20,8	0,06	8,8	165
Beef	18,9	0,0	12,4	187
Pork (not fat)	16,4	0,0	27,8	316
Salmon	20,8	0,0	15,1	219
Tuna	22,7	0,0	0,7	96
Cod	17,5	0,0	0,6	75
Tomatoes	0,6	2,9	-	14
Potatoes	2,0	19,7	0,1	83
Carrot	1,3	7,0	0,1	33
Cabbage	1,8	5,4	-	28
Apples	0,4	11,3	-	46
Oranges	0,9	8,4	-	38

Grape	0,4	17,5	-	69
Cucumber	0,7	1,8	-	10
Mushrooms	3,2	1,6	0,7	25
Lettuce	1,5	2,2	-	14
Parsley	3,7	8,1	-	45
Red pepper	1,3	5,7	-	27
Banana	1,5	22,4	-	91
Beet	1,7	10,8	-	48
Peach	0,9	10,4	-	44
Raspberry	0,8	9,0	-	41
Blueberry	1,0	7,7	-	37
Cherry	0,8	11,3	-	49

Average values are presented here.
Values may vary.

Table of content

Recipe ...   Page

Table of content

Recipe ...

Page

Table of content

Recipe ...   Page

Table of content

Recipe ...   **Page**

Recipe

Cook time

Prep time

Serves

Best served with

Notes

Ingredients

Instruction

Recipe

Cook time

- Prep time

- Serves

- Best served with

Notes

Ingredients

Instruction

Recipe ✍ ....

Cook time ✍ ....

....

Prep time ✍ ....

....

Serves ✍ ....

....

Best served with ✍

....

....

Notes

....

....

....

....

....

Ingredients

....

....

....

....

....

....

Instruction

....

....

....

....

....

....

....

....

Recipe

Cook time

Prep time

Serves

Best served with

Notes

Ingredients

Instruction

Recipe _____

Cook time _____

- _____

Prep time _____

- _____

- _____

Serves _____

- _____

- _____

Best served with

- _____

- _____

Ingredients

- _____ - _____
- _____ - _____
- _____ - _____
- _____ - _____
- _____ - _____
- _____ - _____

Instruction

- _____
- _____
- _____
- _____
- _____
- _____

-
-
-
-
-
-
-
-
-
-
-
-
-
-
-
-

Recipe

Cook time

- Prep time

- Serves

Best served with

-
-

Notes

-
-
-
-
-

Ingredients

-
-
-
-
-
-

-
-
-
-
-
-

Instruction

-
-
-
-
-

Recipe ✍ ....

Cook. time ✍ ....

• ....

Prep. time ✍ ....

• ....

• ....

Serves ✍ ....

• ....

• ....

• ....

Best served with ◄ ....

• ....

• ....

Ingredients

• ....   • ....

• ....   • ....

• ....   • ....

• ....   • ....

• ....   • ....

• ....   • ....

• ....   • ....

Instruction

• ....

• ....

• ....

• ....

• ....

• ....

- ....
- ....
- ....
- ....
- ....
- ....
- ....
- ....
- ....
- ....
- ....
- ....
- ....
- ....
- ....
- ....

Recipe

Cook time

Prep time

Serves

Best served with

Notes

Ingredients

Instruction

- _____
- _____
- _____
- _____
- _____
- _____
- _____
- _____
- _____
- _____
- _____
- _____
- _____
- _____
- _____
- _____
- _____

Recipe

Cook. time

Prep. time

Serves

Best served with

Notes

Ingredients

Instruction

Recipe ⟋

Cook time ⟋
....

• ....

Prep time ⟋
....

• ....

Serves ⟋
....

• ....

Best served with ⟋

....

....

Notes

• ....

• ....

• ....

• ....

• ....

Ingredients

• ....
• ....
• ....
• ....
• ....
• ....

• ....
• ....
• ....
• ....
• ....

Instruction

• ....
• ....
• ....
• ....
• ....
• ....

- —————————————————————————————————————
- —————————————————————————————————————
- —————————————————————————————————————
- —————————————————————————————————————
- —————————————————————————————————————
- —————————————————————————————————————
- —————————————————————————————————————
- —————————————————————————————————————
- —————————————————————————————————————
- —————————————————————————————————————
- —————————————————————————————————————
- —————————————————————————————————————
- —————————————————————————————————————
- —————————————————————————————————————
- —————————————————————————————————————
- —————————————————————————————————————
- —————————————————————————————————————
- —————————————————————————————————————

Recipe _____

Cook time _____

_____

Prep. time _____

_____

_____

Serves _____

_____

_____

Best served with

_____

_____

Ingredients

_____   _____

_____   _____

_____   _____

_____   _____

_____   _____

_____   _____

Instruction

_____

_____

_____

_____

_____

_____

- ....
- ....
- ....
- ....
- ....
- ....
- ....
- ....
- ....
- ....
- ....
- ....
- ....
- ....
- ....
- ....
- ....

Recipe

Cook time

Prep. time

Serves

Best served with

Notes

Ingredients

Instruction

Recipe ....

Cook time ....

Prep. time ....

Serves ....

Best served with

....

....

Ingredients

.... | ....
.... | ....
.... | ....
.... | ....
.... | ....
.... | ....

Instruction

....

....

....

....

....

....

- ....
- ....
- ....
- ....
- ....
- ....
- ....
- ....
- ....
- ....
- ....
- ....
- ....
- ....
- ....
- ....
- ....
- ....

Recipe

Cook time

Prep time

Serves

Best served with

Notes

Ingredients

Instruction

Recipe

Cook time

Prep time

Serves

Best served with

Notes

Ingredients

Instruction

- _____
- _____
- _____
- _____
- _____
- _____
- _____
- _____
- _____
- _____
- _____
- _____
- _____
- _____
- _____
- _____
- _____
- _____

Recipe

Cook time

- Prep time

- Serves

- Best served with

Notes

Ingredients

Instruction

Recipe

Cook time

Prep. time

Serves

Best served with

Notes

Ingredients

Instruction

44

Recipe

Cook time

Prep time

Serves

Best served with

Notes

Ingredients

Instruction

- _____
- _____
- _____
- _____
- _____
- _____
- _____
- _____
- _____
- _____
- _____
- _____
- _____
- _____
- _____
- _____
- _____
- _____

Recipe ....

Cook. time ....

Notes

Prep. time ....

Serves ....

Best served with

Ingredients

Instruction

- _____
- _____
- _____
- _____
- _____
- _____
- _____
- _____
- _____
- _____
- _____
- _____
- _____
- _____
- _____
- _____
- _____

Recipe

Cook time

- ## Prep time

- ## Serves

- ## Best served with

Notes

Ingredients

Instruction

Recipe ✎

Cook time ✎

Prep time ✎

Serves ✎

Best served with ✎

Notes

Ingredients

Instruction

- _____
- _____
- _____
- _____
- _____
- _____
- _____
- _____
- _____
- _____
- _____
- _____
- _____
- _____
- _____
- _____
- _____

Recipe

Cook time

Prep time

Serves

Best served with

Notes

Ingredients

Instruction

Recipe _____

Cook time _____

Notes

• _____

Prep time _____

• _____

• _____

Serves _____

• _____

• _____

Best served with _____

• _____

_____

_____

Ingredients

• _____ • _____

• _____ • _____

• _____ • _____

• _____ • _____

• _____ • _____

• _____ • _____

• _____

Instruction

_____

_____

_____

_____

_____

_____

- _____
- _____
- _____
- _____
- _____
- _____
- _____
- _____
- _____
- _____
- _____
- _____
- _____
- _____
- _____
- _____
- _____

Recipe

Cook time

Prep. time

Serves

Best served with

Notes

- ....
- ....
- ....
- ....
- ....

- ....
- ....

Ingredients

- ....
- ....
- ....
- ....
- ....
- ....

- ....
- ....
- ....
- ....
- ....

Instruction

- ....
- ....
- ....
- ....
- ....

Recipe

Cook time

Prep. time

Serves

Best served with

Notes

Ingredients

Instruction

Recipe

Cook. time

Prep. time

Serves

Best served with

Notes

Ingredients

Instruction

Recipe

Cook time

- ## Prep time

- ## Serves

- ## Best served with

-
-

Notes

-
-
-
-

Ingredients

-
-
-
-
-

Instruction

-
-
-
-
-

Recipe

Cook. time

Prep. time

Serves

Best served with

Notes

Ingredients

Instruction

Recipe

Cook. time

Prep. time

Serves

Best served with

Notes

Ingredients

Instruction

- _____
- _____
- _____
- _____
- _____
- _____
- _____
- _____
- _____
- _____
- _____
- _____
- _____
- _____
- _____
- _____
- _____

Recipe _____

Cook. time _____

Prep. time _____

Serves _____

Best served with _____

Notes

- _____
- _____
- _____
- _____
- _____

Ingredients

- _____   - _____
- _____   - _____
- _____   - _____
- _____   - _____
- _____   - _____
- _____   - _____

Instruction

- _____
- _____
- _____
- _____
- _____
- _____

-
-
-
-
-
-
-
-
-
-
-
-
-
-
-
-
-
-

Recipe

Cook time

Prep. time

Serves

Best served with

Notes

Ingredients

Instruction

Recipe _____

Cook time _____

Prep. time _____

Serves _____

Best served with _____

Ingredients

Instruction

74

- ....
- ....
- ....
- ....
- ....
- ....
- ....
- ....
- ....
- ....
- ....
- ....
- ....
- ....
- ....
- ....
- ....
- ....

Recipe _____

Cook time _____

Prep. time _____

Serves _____

Best served with _____

Notes

Ingredients

Instruction

- _____
- _____
- _____
- _____
- _____
- _____
- _____
- _____
- _____
- _____
- _____
- _____
- _____
- _____
- _____
- _____
- _____

Recipe _____

Cook time _____

Prep time _____

Serves _____

Best served with _____

_____

Notes

· _____
· _____
· _____
· _____
· _____

Ingredients

· _____   · _____
· _____   · _____
· _____   · _____
· _____   · _____
· _____   · _____
· _____   · _____

Instruction

· _____
· _____
· _____
· _____
· _____
· _____
· _____

Recipe

Cook time

- Prep time

- Serves

Best served with

Notes

Ingredients

Instruction

Recipe

Cook time

Prep time

Serves

Best served with

Notes

Ingredients

Instruction

Recipe ....

Cook time ....

Notes

• ....

Prep time ....

• ....

• ....

Serves ....

• ....

• ....

Best served with

• ....

• ....

Ingredients

• .... • ....

• .... • ....

• .... • ....

• .... • ....

• .... • ....

• .... • ....

Instruction

• ....

• ....

• ....

• ....

• ....

• ....

• ....

-
-
-
-
-
-
-
-
-
-
-
-
-
-
-
-
-
-

Recipe

Cook. time

Prep. time

Serves

Best served with

Notes

Ingredients

Instruction

Recipe ....

Cook time ....

Prep time ....

Serves ....

Best served with

Ingredients

Instruction

- _____
- _____
- _____
- _____
- _____
- _____
- _____
- _____
- _____
- _____
- _____
- _____
- _____
- _____
- _____
- _____
- _____
- _____

Recipe

Cook. time

Prep. time

Serves

Best served with

Notes

Ingredients

Instruction

Recipe

Cook time

Prep time

Serves

Best served with

Notes

Ingredients

Instruction

Recipe ✦ ....

Cook. time ✦ ....

• ....

Prep. time ✦ ....

• ....

• ....

Serves ✦ ....

• ....

• ....

• ....

Best served with ✦

• ....

• ....

Ingredients

•	• ....
•	• ....
•	• ....
•	• ....
•	• ....
•	• ....
•	• ....

Instruction

• ....

• ....

• ....

• ....

• ....

• ....

• ....

Recipe ....

Cook time ....

Prep time ....

Serves ....

Best served with

....

....

Notes

....

....

....

....

Ingredients

....

....

....

....

....

....

Instruction

....

....

....

....

....

....

Recipe

Cook. time

Prep. time

Serves

Best served with

Notes

....
....
....
....
....

Ingredients

....
....
....
....
....
....

Instruction

....
....
....
....
....
....

Recipe

Cook time

Prep. time

Serves

Best served with

Notes

Ingredients

Instruction

- ....
- ....
- ....
- ....
- ....
- ....
- ....
- ....
- ....
- ....
- ....
- ....
- ....
- ....
- ....
- ....
- ....

Recipe ✍ ....

Cook. time ✍ ....

Notes

Prep. time ✍ ....

Serves ✍ ....

Best served with ✍

....

....

Ingredients

Instruction

- _____
- _____
- _____
- _____
- _____
- _____
- _____
- _____
- _____
- _____
- _____
- _____
- _____
- _____
- _____
- _____
- _____
- _____

Recipe ✎ ....

Cook time ✎ ....

Prep time ✎ ....

Serves ✎ ....

Best served with ✎

....

....

• ....

• ....

• ....

• ....

• ....

Ingredients

• ....   • ....

• ....   • ....

• ....   • ....

• ....   • ....

• ....   • ....

• ....   • ....

Instruction

• ....

• ....

• ....

• ....

• ....

• ....

• ....

Recipe

Cook. time

Prep. time

Serves

Best served with

Notes

Ingredients

Instruction

Recipe

Cook time

Prep time

Serves

Best served with

Notes

Ingredients

Instruction

- _____
- _____
- _____
- _____
- _____
- _____
- _____
- _____
- _____
- _____
- _____
- _____
- _____
- _____
- _____
- _____
- _____
- _____

Recipe ❧

Cook. time ❧ _____

Prep. time ❧ _____

Serves ❧ _____

Best served with ⬅

_____

_____

Notes

_____
_____
_____
_____
_____
_____

Ingredients

_____ _____
_____ _____
_____ _____
_____ _____
_____ _____
_____ _____

Instruction

_____
_____
_____
_____
_____
_____

- ....
- ....
- ....
- ....
- ....
- ....
- ....
- ....
- ....
- ....
- ....
- ....
- ....
- ....
- ....
- ....
- ....

Recipe

Cook time

-

Prep. time

-

Serves

-

Best served with

-

Notes

-
-
-
-
-

Ingredients

-
-
-
-
-

-
-
-
-
-

Instruction

-
-
-
-
-

Recipe ....

Cook. time ....

Notes

- ....

Prep. time ....

- ....

- ....

Serves ....

- ....

- ....

Best served with

- ....

- ....

Ingredients

- ....   - ....
- ....   - ....
- ....   - ....
- ....   - ....
- ....   - ....

Instruction

- ....
- ....
- ....
- ....
- ....
- ....

Recipe ⟨
Cook time ⟨

Notes

Prep time ⟨

Serves ⟨

Best served with ⟨

Ingredients

Instruction

Recipe

Cook. time

Prep. time

Serves

Best served with

Notes

Ingredients

Instruction

Recipe ✍

Cook time ✍ _____

Notes
❦

- · _____
- · _____

Prep. time ✍ _____

- · _____

Serves ✍ _____

- · _____

Best served with ✍

- · _____
- · _____

Ingredients
❦

- · _____ · _____
- · _____ · _____
- · _____ · _____
- · _____ · _____
- · _____ · _____
- · _____ · _____

Instruction
❦

- · _____
- · _____
- · _____
- · _____
- · _____
- · _____

Recipe ✍ ....

Cook. time ✍ ....

Notes

Prep. time ✍ ....

Serves ✍ ....

Best served with ✍

Ingredients

Instruction

- ⋯
- ⋯
- ⋯
- ⋯
- ⋯
- ⋯
- ⋯
- ⋯
- ⋯
- ⋯
- ⋯
- ⋯
- ⋯
- ⋯
- ⋯
- ⋯
- ⋯

Recipe ✎ ....

Cook time ✎ ....

Prep time ✎ ....

Serves ✎ ....

Best served with ◀
....
....

Notes

• ....
• ....
• ....
• ....
• ....

Ingredients

• .... • ....
• .... • ....
• .... • ....
• .... • ....
• .... • ....
• .... • ....

Instruction

....
....
....
....
....
....
....

Recipe ✍

Cook time ✍

Prep time ✍

Serves ✍

Best served with ✍

Notes

Ingredients

Instruction

Recipe

Cook time

Prep time

Serves

Best served with

Notes

Ingredients

Instruction

-
-
-
-
-
-
-
-
-
-
-
-
-
-
-
-
-

Recipe ≪ ....

Cook. time ≪ ....

Notes

•..

Prep. time ≪ ....

•..

•..

Serves ≪ ....

•..

•..

Best served with ≪

•..

....

....

Ingredients

•..   •..

•..   •..

•..   •..

•..   •..

•..   •..

•..   •..

Instruction

•..

•..

•..

•..

•..

•..

Recipe
Cook. time

Prep. time

Serves

Best served with

Notes

Ingredients

Instruction

Recipe
Cook. time

Notes

Prep. time

Serves

Best served with

Ingredients

Instruction

- ....
- ....
- ....
- ....
- ....
- ....
- ....
- ....
- ....
- ....
- ....
- ....
- ....
- ....
- ....
- ....
- ....
- ....

Recipe

Cook time

Prep time

Serves

Best served with

Notes

Ingredients

Instruction

Recipe ✒

Cook time ✒

Prep time ✒

Serves ✒

Best served with ✒

Notes

Ingredients

Instruction

Recipe

Cook. time

Prep. time

Serves

Best served with

Notes

Ingredients

Instruction

Recipe

Cook. time

Prep. time

Serves

Best served with

Notes

Ingredients

Instruction

Recipe

Cook time

- Prep time

- Serves

Best served with

Notes

Ingredients

Instruction

Recipe

Cook time

Prep. time

Serves

Best served with

Notes

Ingredients

Instruction

Recipe

Cook. time

Prep. time

Serves

Best served with

Notes

Ingredients

Instruction

Recipe ✍ ....

Cook. time ✍ ....

Prep. time ✍ ....

Serves ✍ ....

Best served with ☜

....

....

Notes

....

....

....

....

....

Ingredients

....

....

....

....

....

....

Instruction

....

....

....

....

....

....

Recipe _____

Cook. time _____

Notes

Prep. time _____

Serves _____

Best served with _____

Ingredients

Instruction

Recipe ✍ ....

Cook time ✍ ....

Notes

· ....

Prep time ✍ .... · ....

· ....

· ....

Serves ✍ .... · ....

· ....

· ....

Best served with ✍

· ....

· ....

Ingredients

· .... · ....

· .... · ....

· .... · ....

· .... · ....

· .... · ....

· .... · ....

Instruction

· ....

· ....

· ....

· ....

· ....

· ....

Recipe ✍ ....

Cook time ✍ ....

Notes

....

Prep time ✍ ....

....

....

Serves ✍ ....

....

....

Best served with ◄

....

....

Ingredients

.... | ....

.... | ....

.... | ....

.... | ....

.... | ....

.... | ....

Instruction

....

....

....

....

....

....

- ....
- ....
- ....
- ....
- ....
- ....
- ....
- ....
- ....
- ....
- ....
- ....
- ....
- ....
- ....
- ....
- ....

Recipe

Cook time

Prep time

Serves

Best served with

Notes

Ingredients

Instruction

Recipe

Cook time

Prep time

Serves

Best served with

Notes

Ingredients

Instruction

- _____
- _____
- _____
- _____
- _____
- _____
- _____
- _____
- _____
- _____
- _____
- _____
- _____
- _____
- _____
- _____
- _____

Notes

CPSIA information can be obtained
at www.ICGtesting.com
Printed in the USA
LVHW061726180323
741934LV00027B/795

9 781792 812347